*A Celebration of Community,
Poetry, Art & Wine*

Verse on the Vine™ Anthology

Original Poetry
by
Featured Poets/Performers
of
Verse on the Vine™
2012-2013

Editing & Book Layout:
Shawn Aveningo

Cover Design & Photography:
Robert R. Sanders

Library of Congress Control Number: 2013916910

ISBN-13: 978-0615888255
ISBN-10: 0615888259

Published by The Poetry Box™, 2013
Fair Oaks, California
www.thePoetryBox.com
530.409.0721

*This Collection of Poems is
Dedicated to:*

*all the lovers of poetry,
aspiring writers,
established authors,
open-mic junkies,
clever wordsmiths
and
every humbled soul
who's ever picked up a book
and found themselves
lost in the pages*

TABLE OF CONTENTS

INTRODUCTION

A poet, a painter and a photographer walk into a wine bar…

Sounds like the beginning of an old joke, doesn't it? Instead, it's the beginning of a wonderful journey. The past two years have been just that… a journey.

In November 2011, a friend of mine, Lisa Magruder, an artist whose paintings are displayed at The Wine Gallery, contacted me and told me the new owner, Yvonne Norgauer of Petra Vineyard, was interested in having "some sort of poetry show". I met with Yvonne a few weeks later to discover a wonderful opportunity to bring poetry & spoken word to the historic old town of Folsom, CA. My partner Robert Sanders and I began brainstorming, and a few months later, Verse on the Vine™ was born.

I had spent the last 5 years traveling down from Rescue, CA to Downtown Sacramento to attend a variety of poetry shows, some featuring prominent poets from all over the globe and others whose entertainment came in the form of colorful, often unexpected, open-mic poets. However, every time I invited my friends from "up the hill" to come downtown to a show, many would balk at the distance or the late night start times. So naturally, when the chance to host a series in 'the burbs' arrived, I jumped at the opportunity.

Why Poetry?

I have always believed that poetry is so much more than what is taught in the ivory towers of academia. Art imitates life; life imitates art. And that's exactly how poetry works, blurring the lines between truth and poetic license, to achieve a higher insight.

My goal is to show people that poetry can be fun and entertaining, to bring poetry to the non-poets. I can't even begin to count the number of instances when someone has attended Verse on the Vine™, admitting to me that this was their first ever poetry reading, and then shared with me how much they enjoyed it. They often seem so surprised…and that's always my favorite reaction.

Today, poetry is for everyone. It's meant to tell a story, paint a picture, evoke emotion, cause you to think, enrage you, involve you, and most of all -- move you. It's all these things and more.

We have enjoyed hearing poets from varied backgrounds, young and old, experienced and novice. Some of them have been traditional in their presentation, and some have brought a more urban, youthful vibe to our stage. We've been entertained by poets with banjos, saxophones, cellos and guitars. We've huddled together to hear shocking & poignant stories from a poet in her eighties, who has since passed away. (Patricia Hickerson, you are dearly missed.) We've hooted & hollered to some very sexy erotic verse as well. One thing is for sure – the first amendment is alive and kickin', as all forms of spoken word are welcome at Verse on the Vine™.

A Cornucopia of Talent

When Robert and I decided to bring Verse on the Vine™ to fruition, we knew early on we were fighting an uphill battle. While poetry readings were commonplace in the more urban settings, our suburbanites were not quite as accustomed to attending this type of entertainment. And even though this was exactly the type of event we at The Poetry Box™ wanted to sponsor, we knew we had to book the most talented poetic performers in our region to establish a steady audience. So, that's exactly what we did!

We were lucky to have three Poets Laureate grace our stage and share their poetry. Thank you Bob Stanley, Allegra Silberstein and Jeff Knorr. Your support of our series is appreciated more than you'll ever know.

Our audience has been treated to out-of-town talents, such as Matthew Lane Brouwer from Bellingham, Washington, Todd Cirillo, whose returned to his 'N'awlins' roots, Brigit Truex, whose now a resident poet in Kentucky, and the popular Nevada City syndicated radio poet, Molly Fisk.

We've enjoyed local favorites such as Telemachos Greanias, Jack Donaldson, Phillip Larrea and Stan Zumbiel, and we dared to let our hair down with our erotic poetry nights steaming up the Wine Gallery windows with the sultry verse of NSAA, Kelly Freeman and Poetica Erotica.

We also had the pleasure of witnessing our talented local youth, as the finalist from the El Dorado County Poetry Out Loud Competition shared their individual interpretations of legendary poems for our National Poetry Month show in April.

And who can forget our award-winning poet performers like Indigo Moor, Cynthia Linville, Shawn Pittard, Catherine Fraga, Lytton Bell and Laura Martin. They are some of the most prolific voices in our region and an inspiration to many.

With Much Gratitude

Thank you to all of our featured poets for their hard work, travel, support and contribution to our poetry series, and now this anthology. Without their brilliant talent and commitment to quality writing and showmanship, we would not have a show to produce.

I can't even begin to express enough gratitude for my partner, Robert Sanders. He has put in countless hours designing our promotional posters for each show and memorializing each performer with his photography. Without him, Verse on the Vine™ would not have grown to be the success it is today.

Thank you, Yvonne for your collaboration, for always being the gracious hostess, for making everyone feel welcome and for providing this opportunity to share my passion with the town of Folsom.

And dear reader, I thank you, as well, for your support of our poetic endeavor. I hope this collection of poetry leaves you inspired to further explore this wonderful world we call Poetry...attend a reading, buy a book, write a poem or perhaps even find your own voice as you step up to the open-mic.

~Shawn Aveningo

Shawn Aveningo

February 2012

ANOTHER SIP

Shawn Aveningo

Tender grape
ripened by the sun,
reaches its glory
as it's crushed.

My heart too
has been fermenting,
sometimes lamenting,
over choices of my past,
and pain that seems to last,
as I sip another glass,
and toast "to life".

I take in
the full-bodied bouquet
of motherhood, womanhood,
happiness, pain,
splendor, disappointment,
forgiveness, shame.

And as this tonic teases my tongue,
it releases wonderment,
and wondering…
Is there more?
Should I take another sip?

JUST ANOTHER DAY

Shawn Aveningo

"Must the hunger become anger and the anger fury,
before anything will be done?"
John Steinbeck

Another night of dreams upon corrugated pillows survived,
mother and child in their daily trek to *Loaves and Fishes*,

line stretching 'round a city block. *Escalades* bearing
Jesus Fish, *Little Nemo* displayed on flip down plasmas,

unloading youngsters in tartan skirts & poplin blouses. "Ma'am
could you spare a little change?", echoes from invisible shadows

to those deaf by choice to their cries. The cries of infants,
bellies swollen from hunger, mothers too famished to produce

nature's nourishment, fathers desperate, ashamed. Hunger
to anger. Anger to Fury. Fury to blood spilled on the streets.

Public outcries as pie charts in papers show crime on the rise.
It's November. Politicians' promises tallied. Soon after bells ring,

coins collect in red buckets, 'tis the season for giving. Until
Spring cleaning sweeps poverty under the rug and CPA's tally

charity on Schedule A's. Just another day in paradise.

FAVORITE SKIES {*for Robert*}

Shawn Aveningo

He'd often tell me how he loved the sky.
Look, he would say, look at the glorious pastels
painted across the atmosphere.
See how they dance, these viscous wisps in the wind
ever changing, calling out to us to take a quick peek
before they vanish into the sky's next song.
This was my favorite sky.

I imagine him as a small boy,
running up and down the grass covered hillsides,
singing and dancing, without a stitch of clothes,
or a care to burden him, twirling round and round
in circles, until in dizzy defiance he'd collapse.
I imagine him lying there, the sky spinning above him,
the shift-shaping clouds, his new best friends.
Perhaps this, his favorite sky.

Hand in hand we walk to the market. He stops us
dead in our tracks. Look. Just look at that sunset,
how perfectly the pink morphs into peach
with a streak of violet to punctuate its splendor.
Dinner that evening tasted especially fine
and the love we made was delicious.
This, my new favorite sky.

He held my hand at Joshua Tree, the night
the lunar man chose to hide his face.
Look, he said. See the trillions of stars
twinkling as brilliant as your smile.
A chill lingered just long enough
in the space between our embrace,
capturing my breath writing out his name,
like wispy white smoke rings in an ebony night.
Forever our favorite sky.

Bob Stanley

March 2012

PILGRIMAGE
On Taking the Fourth Grade to Malakoff Diggins

Bob Stanley

Smooth pink
limbs, this thin-skinned
Manzanita will survive
leave its dead brush behind.

We sense incense cedar up close, but
mountain misery
kitkitdizze
smells strong like
witch hazel if you rub it
thumb to forefinger
clears the head.

Passing the stick
around the circle
in China Garden
we feel in the sunshine
those unnamed miners
beneath the apple blossoms -
it is May on the Mountain.

These wolves and rabbits play tag
learning how to be prey
and preyed upon, the children
run faster, widening the circle.

Mountain guide (we call him "one-eye")
tells a tale: Tibetan climbers
saw a halo in the sky
so beautiful, they leapt
into its void of color and light.

As we climb the last steep pitch,
thunder rolls. Thirty kids start screaming and run to us

as we hand out tube tents, laugh as they
try to assemble their homes as white hail fills the camp.

Cold feet, cold hands at dinner
washing dishes in hot water.

Sugar pine, Manzanita
prepared for the fire.

STILL WORKING

Bob Stanley

Grey-faced
owl bursts from the beech
flies three circles above us
to sweep off towards the
riffle and roar of the River G.

Great blue takes off at
midnight, New Year's,
high above us, red wine
spilled on brown rug:
your children will run
along these streets.
Firecrackers.

Five a.m. rainsplash hard outside;
I fall back to bed, and you,
unknowing
wrap yourself around me like night
and we swirl
deeper than we knew
words making little sense
on a page, but still working
on timing
not stopping
like laughter.

RAM DASS SPEAKS IN THE VALLEY

Bob Stanley

As bright as the forehead of sky
my distant land sings
the song of the goddess of winds of the world

I approach you with care
knowing I will hurt you, forest;
I break a twig.

Kabir said
want to be a poet?
burn your house!

For centuries we have fought each other
and we are happy
and we have almost nothing

Lost in the wilderness
the yaks are the ones
with the longest coats

We forget how critical is the tongue
the infinite rolling of R
T – the touch of the teeth

I will take my time
to hold language in my mouth
to make song

ROSEVILLE, CA

Bob Stanley

Was it roses instead of people that lived here
like Orangevale was oranges
and Citrus Heights – lemons maybe?

What could be more sweet?
Was it open fields of them?
Did God prune them back in January
and then watch them bloom from May to November the
way California's endless summer just lets them bloom – roses flaring
heedless toward the edge of winter?

Did folks coming in from East detrain at Roseville station
and smell the fragrant perfume of the place?
Where mountain and valley meet? Do they still?

Before there was a railroad, there was the land,
says the city website
mile after mile of waving grasslands.

Oaks of course, *quercus lobata* all down the slope,
poppies, lupine and lilies and alongside the streams'
shady banks the wild roses in their delicate pale shades.

So there were roses
and now there're roses on signs and roses in yards
and in the words
so the people are the flowers now
waiting for the train or the sign that reminds them of
who they are and what land they stand on
alongside the track by the old road they still gather
believing in roses, impossible roses.

Cynthia Linville

April 2012

SHE HAS HER REASONS

Cynthia Linville

She dreams of a letter she'll never send
written in cuneiform
the stylus pressing so precisely
into wet clay from
top to bottom
again and again.

She dreams of writing her autobiography
focusing on the moment
she decides to turn right
at the white tree
to go into the old cabin and
face her enemy.

She dreams of empty rooms
behind closed doors
of cleaned out closets
and holes in floors
that spew smoke,
tiny bits of glass, and feathers.

The ghost of a thumbnail moon
illuminates these detours
of her restless night.
When she awakes
all that remains
are cobwebbed doorways.

PERSEVERATION

Cynthia Linville

The fig tree leans into the water
kissing again and again
this blue, this green

The wind sings into the storm
crying again and again
let her go, better go

His fingers return to the scar
caressing again and again
left to right, right to left

The crows' silence gets into his dreams
warning again and again
danger, time to leave

THEY NEVER ONCE MADE IT TO VALENTINE'S DAY

Cynthia Linville

The wind sings just like a ghost, invisible.
It belongs to her.

I'm exactly where I want to be, he said defensively.
It all comes down to relentless ultimatums.

The horizon is straight and blue –
no one else sees it but her.

She was in love with him even then,
even when *always beautiful* was just not enough,
was entangled with angels.

What they thought was a candle burning
turned out to be a pile of broken glass.

She needed more.
What can be restored without stripping the core?

* * *

What can be restored without stripping the core?
It belongs to her.

The horizon is straight and blue,
was entangled with angels
even when *always beautiful* was just not enough.

She needed more.

What they thought was a candle burning
turned out to be a pile of broken glass.
(She was in love with him even then.)
No one else sees it but her –

27

the wind sings just like a ghost, invisible.
I'm exactly where I want to be, he said defensively.
It all comes down to relentless ultimatums.

* * *

It all comes down to relentless ultimatums.
What they thought was a candle burning
turned out to be a pile of broken glass –

It belongs to her.
I'm exactly where I want to be.

He said, defensively,
she needed more,
was entangled with angels.

She was in love with him even then.

The horizon is straight and blue,
even when *always beautiful* was just not enough.

(No one else sees it but her.)

The wind sings just like a ghost, invisible.
What can be restored without stripping the core?

Patricia Hickerson

May 2012

18 km WEST OF VARNA

Patricia Hickerson

At Pobiti Kamani
ancient site of oracles
she doesn't remember a
dry plain of underwater stones
only a sway of delicate birch trees
forested in the yellow sand of Black Sea soil.

Becalmed among the dappled spirits
she heard them sigh
in the language of Bulgaria.
She was quieted anyway.

SPANISH INFLUENZA 1919

Patricia Hickerson

they were sick as dogs 14-yr-old Edith and Mama but
not Papa or little Bobby who was 3. After they recovered
Mama took Edith and Bobby on the train from Oklahoma City
down to Aunt Julia's Texas ranch.
It was there on the afternoon of a tornado at least it looked like
there might be a tornado
sky all yellow with sulphur flashes some lightning they huddled in
the storm cellar
Edith let out an ear-splitting scream said she'd seen a rattler coiled
on a ledge above
My, what a scream to come out of a scrawny teenaged girl
Why Edith, you must be imagining things
but it was true one of the hired hands saw it, too, said he was going
to have a
wrestling match with the snake he reached up, Edith screamed again
then Aunt Julia said leave the snake alone we are going back to the
house
Edith told Mama the snake stared at her that he had eyes like
Papa's, always
staring at her Mama said don't be silly
Next morning Edith was in the bathhouse, saw another snake coiled
on a ledge
went screaming naked as a jaybird into Aunt Julia's kitchen
why she still ain't got no titties, cackled someone's aged grandma
sucking on her corncob
pipe rocking on the back porch
everybody laughed to see Edith, lanky as a winter tree, still no tits!

back home in Oklahoma City, Mama decided to take Bobby back to
Kentucky
to show off her beautiful child to her mother and her sisters
leaving Edith alone in the house with Papa one morning he was
standing in her bedroom
doorway looking at her as she lay under the covers
she knew what was going to happen

drew the covers up tight under her chin
didn't matter
decided she would scream bloody murder loud enough for the
neighbors to hear
and Papa would leap from her bed undone
as though he had never been there
and that's what happened

when Mama came back from Kentucky Edith told her what Papa had
tried to do
Mama just said "awww" and pushed the air with her open hand as
though what can
you expect from a man like that who won't even take care of his
family a man who stands
on the street corner all day long jawing with his cronies

but it didn't mean Edith stopped loving Papa after all he was her
father
he'd given her a cameo ring for her 12th birthday
(where'd you get the money for that, Mama stormed)
one morning brought her a tumbler of whisky saying this'll put hair
on your chest
Edith made a face at the smell turned on her pillow Take it away,
Papa

RED HOT

Patricia Hickerson

it was still morning
and he began to burn
in a room of many windows
looking out on a side street of the city

watched her with those shoes
she was barefoot in jeans
and a flowered pajama top
flowers red as a cat's tongue
as though she had just hopped out of bed
husband a minus since dawn
they were gold spike-heeled sandals
she held them in her lap
played with the straps
as she might play with any man
her hands small, fingers tender soft

in the room a brown leather couch
an upright piano, stool to whirl
a TV set on a bench
a chair upholstered green
where he chose to sit
after she answered the door
and invited him in

she took in his rap
from a deeper chair
where she nestled careless
her scorched honey hair kicking back
across the cushion
turned toward him, gave him the once-over
he began to burn

it would happen that night
they would meet on a corner

the flowers on her pajama top still red
red as a cat's tongue, that's what she was
a kitten he could throw high in the air
catch in his arms when she fell,
and he would explore her
find her parts as hot as a killer's tongue
pulsing blood-red as last night's sunset.

Allegra Silberstein

May 2012

IN DIFFUSED LIGHT

Allegra Silberstein

A piece of paper, a scatter of ink,
messages, like bridges we cross,
water below, blue sky above
spanning channels of gain and loss.
Outside the room, trees tangle thoughts:
their falling leaves, their golden flight:
butterflies weaving in and out
flowering is diffused morning light
without shadows and magic glows,
wraps a theurgy on my heart.
This divine waking on me bestows
new beginnings, a fresh start:
the old words and songs I've sung
come to poems I've just begun.

MY JOSEPH

Allegra Silberstein

We envied you, the youngest,
as if you had been singled out
for a coat of many colors.
We said Mom spoiled you.

We were wrong.
Love made you strong.
You grew to manhood with courage
enough to hold at bay

the gnawing years that would
chew upon the heart remorselessly,
the way packs of wild dogs
devour the downed lamb.

You stayed with Mom and Dad—
held back the dark
that folded in on the farm,
held fast to our mother.

You stayed to tend the fields,
to mind the cattle and we were free
to leave: to embroider our garments
with threads of red and gold.

You stayed,
steadfast in your faded coat.

TOWARD GALAXIES

Allegra Silberstein

Breathe
into spirit.
Let the body move
into dance,
creation spiraling
toward galaxies
where colors spin:
a kaleidoscope,
a starry night.

Enter the unknown:
the quest for meaning.
Parameters of the body
will anchor your search
with understanding
held in the genes
ancient as Abraham.

Take your soul by the
hand and let it touch
the beaten heart,
let it feel the soft
wind's whisper.
The breath.
The body.

OLD WOMAN WITH SPRINGTIME EYES

Allegra Silberstein

I remember you:
busy at simple tasks
your dustpan flashing
through sun-glinting particles
as if gathering stardust.

I followed you:
climbed the orchard hill with you.
Afternoon light wrapped 'round us
as we filled our baskets
with red and gold of autumn apples.

Remember you:
in your long green gown.
Shadowed in purple twilight
you watered young plants
with a rusted sprinkler.

Always
I remember your springtime eyes
that bid me welcome—
that lighted my way
when I needed to leave.

Jack Donaldson

June 2012

THE SHAWL

Jack Donaldson

I wrap myself
In life's tattered shawl
Its weight painfull
Bending me
To a stoop

I once wrapped myself
In its comfort
Beauty
Warmth

Now
Coarse
Frayed
And
Threadbare

It is
Penetrated
By
Life's chill

I pull it
Tightly
About my body
It is all
That I own

WHISPERS

Jack Donaldson

I Have
For Many Summers
Sat On A Lover's Carved Bench
Beneath The Cautious Cool Canopy
Of Her Shade

And Listened
To The Breeze Kissed
Whispered Tales
Of Men Who Lusted
For Her Luscious Fruit
The Strength Of Her Limbs

Men Who's Only Desire
To Strip Her
Of Her Fine Timber
And Shape It
To Their Image

She Rooted Here
Long Ago
In This Harsh Stony Soil
Spreading Tender Tendrils
Seeking Nourishment
Inhaling The Exhalations
Of Lovers And The Scorned
As They Sat On This Scared Bench

I Have Shared
As Many Autumns
Watching Children Play
In The Piles
Of Restless Rusting Refuge
She Lays At Her Feet
In Preparation

For Winter's Bitter Chill

And Listened
While She Moaned
In Languished Sleep
Under Ice And Snow's
Frigid Burdens

I Sit Quietly There
Wrapped Against Winter's Harshness
And Marvel At
Her Strength
Her Silhouetted Dignity

I Anxiously Sit
In Spring's Bathing Kiss
As She Draws Her First Breaths
Renewed Life Bursting
From Her Swollen Buds

And I Smile
When Her Joyful
Dew Kissed Leaves
Brush My Cheek
As She Whispers

"Hello Again
My Friend."

Telemachos Greanias

July 2012

SKIVIES

Telemachos Greanias

What's all the fuss about underwear?
There's no real need, nor,
Excuse for them at all.
Yeah, I know about mother's
And, their hospital warnings,
But, who at the ER,
would really give a crap?
I've heard that nuns go commando,
Never heard why, but, so what?

Maybe once we left,
our natural naked state,
we just went nuts
laying on the fabric
to cover what we all know is there.
Gals, and, their fellas,
Spend big bucks on itty-bitty undies
at Victoria's and knock-offs,
but, for what?
Just to get naked again.

Being a mature guy,
I remember windy days,
Ones before panty hose,
When the standard issue
of panty colors was pink, white,
or, none at all!
I recall Lucy Jones in Jr. High
taking a pee in a field
just by hiking her skirt
and bending over.

But social convention rules, I guess,
So, Wal-Mart, here I come, but,
Jockeys, and, only in white!

Hey, know what stretches your skivies?

45

COLOR STREAM

Telemachos Greanias

I strung the Christmas tree lights
across the streamlet,
running an extension to the cabin.
A folding lawn chair came next,
and, I sat,
waiting for the dim,
listening to birds,
as graduated hues,
turned darker.
At dark,
I connected the line.
Brilliance of color came to life
reflecting further off the streamlet,
and, seemed to hesitantly,
flow with the waters movement.
I died that night,
taking the colors,
with me into the ever.

Lytton Bell

August 2012

CAT HOSPITAL

Stopped at the intersection of Manzanita and Cypress
right before you get to the grocery store on the right
I saw them
in the parking lot of the little blue cat hospital
sobbing, embracing
The man: young, bearded, in a blue baseball cap
The woman: also young, chubby, with long, dark, wavy hair
They were both in shorts
They leaned into each other, like uprooted trees, naked roots
tangling
They swayed there, tenuous, propping each other up
and their cat was dead

And I felt an immediate pang of empathetic loss for this anonymous
couple
and I thought about my own cat, advancing in years
grossly obese, diabetic, flea-ridden, nearly toothless
one of my life's few grand, enduring loves
and a gust of relief rushed over me
Today, it is not me bawling in the parking lot
between the ARCO station and the Taco Bell
Just for today, I have escaped that awful, inevitable fate

"What will we do?" I know the woman must have asked the man
who could only shrug, feeling that a new kitten too soon would be
a sign of disloyalty
and I know that they continued embracing
throughout the rest of that day
as they returned to their empty house or apartment
to the silent scratching post
the litter box still full of hard, tiny round turds
cat bed in the corner, covered with white hair
a catnip mousy toy, missing one eye
still, deathlike, on the linoleum
beside a blue dish of half-eaten, fish-flavored food

Loss is the price for loving
and Love, our only solace, rubs its head against us
come what may
It winds itself around our legs, purring
It sleeps beside us
It wakes beside us

I BURIED YOUR LETTERS TODAY

Lytton Bell

You didn't come home last night
In your note dated 1996, you wrote:
"You give me something to look forward to every day.
I love you so much it hurts from head to toe.
My love for you will never change."

In 1997 you wrote: "All I want is
to grow old with you and watch our life together unfold,
watch as our dreams come true one by one. Let me love you
forever."
You sent me roses nine times. I saved every card.
We celebrated five anniversaries and five Christmases together.
You gave me the Heimlich Maneuver once
after which I referred to you as "my hero,"
But you could not save me from drowning; you never even tried
And every word in all your notes:
you lied, you lied, you lied

We honor the dead
We place them in the ground
We cover them with soil to keep them safe
We send them back to God
Over your words, I now say a few words of my own
to seal the deal, to ritualize the letting go:

For all the times we let each other down
For all the times I couldn't get your dick hard
For all the times you couldn't understand my poems
For all the apple pies I fucked up
I was only trying to please you
For the all the stains I washed out of your underwear
For all the times I put up with your family
or helped you with your homework
(How did we let it die? Why did we let it die?)
For all of these reasons

I commend these missives to the earth
When you were sick, I held you
and all the voices of my body told me
"This is your mate. Treat him with infinite tenderness."
All of the small, dark voices of my body love you
They cannot yield
And so, into the ground they must go
I will bury them with you
I will bury every part of myself that still wants you
And then whatever is left can walk away

FUCK YOU, DONNA REED!

Lytton Bell

I can't look at it without guilt
It sits on the shelf in its pretty, unopened box, waiting
my Proctor Silex, 5-speed electric hand mixer
given as a wedding gift in 2002
never touched

Everyone knows I can't cook
From the chocolate chip omelets
I tried to fry for my parents when I was ten, or the banana meatloaf
to the gravy that hardened into a biscuit when I dumped
rather than sifted in the flour
to the apple pie crust which ballooned into a bubble too large
for my oven to contain (an inundation of egg white)
I read the recipes (I do!), but still imagine
I know better

I do not know better

So now my poor children are being brought up on soup and
sandwiches
microwaved pancakes, granola bars and lean cuisine
I flip past the food network, quick as a housefly
careful never to lock eyes with Rachel Ray

Why does this bother me so much?
After all, I am a liberated woman, a feminist
And what is the value of being chained to your stovetop night and
day?
But a secret spite roils in my stomach
when I witness the smug smiles of those who love to cook
whose cooking "relaxes them"
whose delicious dishes are not chores, but works of art

Fuck you, Donna Reed!
Fuck everyone who is good at the things I suck at
I curse you all

And in the hot oven of my envy

a dark cookie of malice blackens on the bottom
and the timer ding

Brigit Truex

September 2012

OLD BARNS
Maysville, Kentucky

Brigit Truex

What shades layer within weathered wood? Burnished pewter,
umber oxide of spring-rusted nails, bleeding streaks against
the eaves' long shadows. Studded with random mud-cups,
swift-refuges from wet and wind. Beneath tin peak,
geometry of a painted quilt-block in blue, red, yellow --
a mirror held up to the moon's radiance. Across the silvered
space, dazzled moths dance with stars, tango with bats that spill
from wide slats, past late-harvest tobacco, its crepe paper leaves.

FIVE GRAYS

Brigit Truex

five gray kits appear from earth, mottled
with dust and lace-shadow, slow heat of late day
fur tipped red taking its color from banded sand-stone
far from here a memory-shade of journeys
like imaginings, someone else's

five grays tumble, pause and peer through bent
frames of stalky grass -- bone-brittle, pale as moon --
their skittish dance a tangle of limbs, black-tipped tail-fluff
then they are gone like dandelion-seed on wind
leaving their elegant grins behind

NOTES AT DAWN AND DUSK

Brigit Truex

At dawn's edge, heron
steps into pond of black silk.
Water heals itself.

October 2012

Poetica Erotica

August 2013

HOW TO SEDUCE ME

Cynthia Linville

I would die for this saxophone
singing through the wrong side of the fence,
bending just so
practically sitting on my lap.
Bitter-tongued kiss
smudged eyes
smeared lipstick –
already too hot to even look at.
All I can think about is this hand
slowly lowering each strap.
Oh yes
make me believe there is a God.
Keep playing.
I desire nothing more
than to disappear into your song.

THE FIRST TIME

Cynthia Linville

You tried so hard to make me cum –
with your fingers, with your tongue
in the backseat of your silver Impala

that you didn't realize it later when you actually did –
standing chest-deep in Folsom Lake
on a church youth outing.

You pulled aside the crotch of my modest one-piece
and shoved your swim-suit-covered penis up into me.

My horizon tilted.

I must have cried out
arched backwards
lost my grip on you.

When I came to, I saw fear in your eyes.
"Are you OK?" you asked.

I must have been loud enough to wake the youth pastor
twenty yards away on the shore.

He looked annoyed
and waved us back
to base camp.

HOW TO SEDUCE ME

Shawn Aveningo

Forget the restaurant.
Forget reservations
    at Zagat's number one pick.
Cook for me.
Prepare my favorite dinner.
Here's a hint…I love Pork.

Forget the Wine.
Forget your collection of vintage cabernet.
The good years are hard enough
  to remember,
    and I really don't wanna work that hard.

Pour me a glass of iced tea.
And let me watch.

Drop six ice-cubes
  into a tall slender glass,
    slippery, cold and wet.
Slowly pour your specialty brew:
  oolong black spice.
Let it slip, slide, slosh, mingle,
  flirting with each cube,
    melting…melting.

And Baby,
no need to add a spoonful of sugar.
I got the honey right here.

HIS ABERRATION

Shawn Aveningo

Scent of her sex wafting
beneath the muggy moonlight
proved to be intoxicating,
irresistible to a lonely traveler
winding his way wistfully
through the maw of New Orleans.

She-devil in fishnets
undresses him, possesses him,
his clerical chastity collar
flung to the floor in fury.

Beads upon her rosary
fingered one by one.
His cock, a pawl against her cunt,
grinds the forbidden fruit.

Baptized anew,
awash in her holy water,
his former faith merely a wraith.
Smoke rings float over his sin,
halos from a cigarette
stained with cherry lipstick.

Todd Cirillo

November 2012

SHAMELESS SELF-PROMOTION

Todd Cirillo

I gave her a magnet
with a poem of mine on it,
titled,
"Riding Giants."
She put it into
her bra.
I thought that was fitting--
then I thought
of when she is at home
later this evening
when her boyfriend
begins to kiss her
and takes her shirt off
and I fall out--
I thought that
was fitting too.

IT DOESN'T TAKE MUCH

Todd Cirillo

When she texted me,
"I kinda miss you,"
I told her
she made my day.

She replied,
"Is it that easy?"

I said,

"It is.
With you."

ALL OF MY FAVORITE THINGS

Todd Cirillo

Upon returning
from one of my many adventures,
without her,
she asked me,
half obligated, half interested,
to tell her what I did
while I was away.

I recounted stories
filled with music,
drinking, dancing,
laughter and
writing poems
next to the Mississippi River.

She walked slightly
behind me
and said,
"well, you were
surrounded by all
of your favorite things."

Catching the hint
of sadness
I told her,
"everything except you"

as she
caught up to me
smiling.

Phillip Larrea

November 2012

LAKE TAHOE, 2004

Phillip Larrea

Violin
Old vine twist
Reminisce

Piano
Naughty pine
Wine sins then

Saxophone
Flight willow
Antique bind

SO UNFAIR

Phillip Larrea

So unfair
That something
In the air

Or water
Or sunlight
Or beauty

Or the pills
Or their men-
Kills women.

ALLEGRA

Phillip Larrea

Allegra.
Senior chick.
Sexy still.

Eighty-two.
Out dancing.
In birkies.

Eats yogurt,
Red meat. Drinks
Sun sweet tea.

TOOTHPASTE MAN - HAIKU

Phillip Larrea

Famous toothpaste man
Squeezed from bottom to top, then
Gets his head lopped off.

Jeff Knorr

February 2013

SACRIFICE {for my son}

Jeff Knorr

It's the jungle and the hot
sun is being cooled
by large palmated leaves.
You and I stand in front of the pyramid
steps and we imagine life then,
what might have happened,
flaying someone open at the top
like field dressing a deer, the leader
lifting out the heart as an offering.
No, it probably didn't happen like that,
these Mayans were peaceful people.

Later that evening at a restaurant table
in a little fishing village you sat
with your mother and I drawing the whole scene.
Sacrifice. You'll understand it someday—
but you're not supposed to just yet.
It's not like standing in the drifting snow
splitting wood because we need more fire.
It's not even like wanting to buy you
that new fishing rod for Christmas
in the window down at Sullivan's Sporting Goods.

No, it's because today the sun is out,
there's a little breeze off the water
and we stand here drifting little midge
patterns to trout. And when I look at you
I think the day couldn't be any better.
It's because, if I do it, everything
might just be a little more beautiful.

FIRST SPRING FISHING

Jeff Knorr

The Walker River is running cold enough that even
the big German Brown trout move dumbly as cattle.
The sun is baking the wild sage into a pungent
oily breeze that keeps me from staying warm today.
What, besides the blood inside me, will vanish if my body
turns to ashes and drifts to the moon?
The birds keep the afternoon humming along
like the shiny Buick's radio running down Hwy 395.
The river bends below me and slows into an emerald slick
before dropping down the canyon on its run to Nevada.
There is a coyote running inside me I cannot find;
it bothers me that I don't know why he is here.
All day I will fight the wind looking for lost lovers and
my grandfather who taught me to sling flies.
By dusk, the moon will watch us, the new season
so worn into me that my ears hiss like the tumbling water
with the distant memory of snow and death and so many goodbyes.

TAKING LEAVE

Jeff Knorr

At the train station in Sacramento,
the young veteran is on his way home
for leave after a long stay in Iraq,
and this valley seems so distant now
from his reality, he goes straight to telling
me of patrols, of tracer fire, of one bright
afternoon in Mosul when his Humvee rocked
with concussion like the sky had imploded.
They had just entered the plaza on a Wednesday
near 11, late morning, people making their market runs
and in the center of this roundabout was a fountain
and on the sidewalks he noticed a young woman
with her small boy and she was kneeling,
wiping something from his chin and he could see
her mouth moving saying something sweetly
to him, not yelling or reprimanding, and it had reminded him
of shopping with his own mother; and then he
noticed an old woman haggling at a stand
selling papers and books and she was shaking
her head and fingers at the old man.
Across the plaza, a young man driving
the small Opel entered the roundabout,
and he passed the young woman wiping her
boy's chin, then he sent a prayer out like a thousand birds
screaming until the plaza and the roundabout became
chaos of smoke and glass, of bodies and car parts.
The Humvee on its side, the soldier crawls out
and begins looking for his platoon members,
and then the woman with the boy, and they are gone.
He can not find her or the small boy, and there is
glass everywhere, glass like jewels scattered among feet.

And now, I'm thinking of you, and how I felt
in the bright Saturday sun looking at photos—
one of me holding the dog we shared, another

of you jumping in my arms in my brother's yard,
and the shrapnel of divorce tears through me,
the phantom limb of you, the field amputation,
holding a piece of your body because I might
find you belong to it. And then I think about this
young man's world exploding and you must have
felt this way the day I broke your heart,
like I had walked with a suicide belt of C-4
into our living room, your limbs going cold,
the lights extinguished; only tears and darkness survived.

What is war but counting bodies?
This is about casualties and making our way back.
There is no returning to the same home on leave.
The ceiling fan is batting overhead
like chopper blades and the land has changed.
Everything familiar here has taken on a new shape
and this evening fades to the flat gun-metal gray of memories.
This young soldier and I sit on our bench awaiting the train.
We are looking for the color of a new country,
for the curve of hills and valleys, for blue rivers'
peace running easy like our hearts.

Indigo Moor

April 2013

Accompanied by Gerry Pineda

LAST CALL IMPROV

Indigo Moor

My apology melts into vodka
and swirling ice. Her fingers lost,
trace the links of her necklace.

On stage, Cecil Taylor cuts heads
with his quartet. Atonal waves plug
the silences in our last dinner together;

two cliff divers on a dizzying drop
from grace. A rapid descent key change
closes her eyes. Cecil's fingers dig

into a flat *B*, drag us into the rhythm.
*Remember when Cecil played that set
at* Smoke's *in the City?*

My breath grazes her ear as she
leans away into stage light glare.
That wasn't him.

Cecil's fingers duel with ivory.
Keys obey. Heart pulp and blood fruit
stain the Steinway's checkered grin.

Her hand slips away as adagio
moves to allegro. Bass player growls
his wide-legged stance.

On the table, my returned key
is a whale beached beyond
the sweat of her glass.

The rhythm leans us into calypso.
Cecil stomps fire wood to wood, kicks
out the back wall, blacks out the sun.

Twenty years ago, she wore black silk.
I kissed her in a field before a rise
of quail against burnt red clouds.

Cecil curled smooth as incense from
my radio as we teased the xylophone
of each other's spine. The drummer

hits a trip wire, drags me away from
shrapneled memories. We snap
our fingers to the deep sweetness

trapped in our skin. There are still no
words we share. A tear rolls down her cheek.
She wipes it away before I can.

ALL WE KNOW

Indigo Moor

This is how the heart turns
On you: the weight of broken vows
Cracks the walls, the throat swells
Into a sun baked highway.
And everything bows to this song.

Isn't it strange
How the softness in a woman's eyes
Can break a neck, weigh a man's
Head to his chest?

We could try again, but there's
No end to some Blues. Platitudes,
A weak glissando; Opening my chest
To the hollow whistling of regret

The taxi's headlights never soon enough.
Shadows flee the gutter and scurry
Beneath her suitcase, buoying it into the trunk.
Lord, don't let her turn around. Don't let her…

Fuck it.
Honey, come on back, let's drag another
Tune from Sisyphus's horn. Until our lips
Splinter and crack against the reed.
Until the drunken sunset staggers off
And trips over the horizon's edge.

ONE SUMMER

Indigo Moor

I could only hold
my children in poems.
I thought
      us cursed, a witch
tormenting our name.

Scoliosis
           rioted
along my youngest
daughter's spine. I slept
for a week beneath

grey walls and ceilings,
      seven sunsets
          spiraling
over the horizon. While

in another room
my oldest daughter, son
          sliced from her,
shuffled gingerly

as if over coals
      and broken glass
from bed to bathroom

holding her belly
          , both our hearts
in such small hands.

Shrunken into a corner,
      my son— he
and his guitar strapped
to a long-sung tonality
trying to ratchet

down a single note
                    for loneliness.

In my worst dreams
we are Icarus, winging
across a rusted desert.

Next scene, they
                    are gut-shot—
one, two, three
black wings flailing

          against broken air,
composite
                    scream vibrating
through my bones.

I turn, not looking
                    and leap, hoping
to be Father-God-Savior

but I carry two
                    cursed hands
that can't possibly hold
          the explosions
blossoming in my chest.

In my best dreams
our fingernails
                    actually touch
before we all fall.

Sophie Meyer

Connor Rickets

Rebecca Dolan

Poetry Out Loud

April 2013
El Dorado County Finalists

Laura Martin

June 2013

THE BODY IS A SOUL SUITCASE

Laura Martin

He buried the cat
sat us down on the couch
explained—briefly—God's will, etc.
bowed head
closed eyes
recited the Lord's Prayer
asked if we had questions
(we had none)
told us to leave that part of the back yard alone
then, forbade crying
deemed it selfish
to want the dead back—
to coax them out of
no more pain no more hardship
no more worries
Someday, he said
we will all be so lucky.

WEEKENDS, EARLY RISER

Laura Martin

Brave the flight
out of your warm, disheveled nest—
the sun is just beginning
to lift its chin
over the mountains
you cannot see from here,
the unbearable chatter of daylight
is still just a whisper,
and it doesn't smell like city yet.
If we go now
we can sneak the first footprints
across frosty lawns
turn cartwheels on lonesome sidewalks
leave love letters in empty mailboxes
before the newspaper hits the porch
before the cats have found
their way back home
from night-prowling.

KETCHUP {for Pat Schneider}

Laura Martin

Made palatable the unpalatable
made eatable the uneatable...
Allowed us to create the Red Sea
on dinner plate nightly
and part it with every food
deemed dipable,
blowed life back into the dry, gritty meatloaf
the too-hard scrambled egg
the fatty gray pork chop—
Served as sweet vinegar salty baptismal
to the breaded and perfectly rectangular fish stick
the once-frozen, squatty Tater Tot
the Ore-Ida crinkle cut French fry—
Salvaged the soul of the Crisco-fried
black iron-skilleted hockey-puck hamburger
the instant mashed potato mountain
otherwise left to drown beneath giant dollops
of easy-spread margarine
and several aluminumed sections of the occasional
Hungry Man TV Dinner—
It had its own sacred place at
the center of the kitchen table, every meal.
It rose high above the salt and pepper shakers
the mismatched serving bowls
the square paper napkin stack
the Melmac plate cradling Safeway brand dinner rolls—
A half-empty glass bottle
with fridge-sweaty wrinkled label
white cap and gaping mouth fused together
with the sticky dark scab of aging tomato squish.
We surrounded our meals with our heads bowed,
our hands clasped under our chins knuckle-white tight,
my father's voice boomed over our heads—

"Dear heavenly father, we thank you
for this meal which we are about to receive."

Catherine Fraga

June 2013

BRAIDED LIVES

Catherine Fraga

"Maybe I enjoy not-being as much as being who I am."
—Stanley Kunitz

This is not an accident:
I find a tooth in a pocket of asphalt
winking at me like a new quarter and
as I bend to claim it I hear
my mother's voice like a familiar blanket
settling in my brain saying it's a fine line a very
thin fine line between the lucky and the
not-so-lucky because this tooth
large adult dull-white
has a story and it begins with a woman
in a budget motel just off some highway
room 16 at the far end of the parking lot boasting
a view of the Beacon station she is wearing
only underwear only a faded mint green slip she leans
up against a quilted dingy beige headboard
a plastic cup of ice pressed against one eye
the eye that is swollen shut with purple bruises
some game show is on the television but she is
not listening the painting above the dresser
reminds her of a jewelry box her aunt gave her
on her ninth birthday painted with white and
yellow daisies a field so thick with color you could
probably hide from someone for a long time
which reminds her to check the door once more
yes it's locked presses a finger into the bloody
hole in her gum lights another cigarette
this slight shadow of a woman whose life
for a moment has postponed my own.

HOLY ART

Catherine Fraga

In 1949 my parents were in love
living on East 14th in a cramped
stucco walkup, above Manuel Lopez
an artist who painted holy cards on
stiff, pale blue paper,
using dimestore watercolors.

I can guess why he did it.
My mother's hair was the color of chestnuts.
Soft, spongy, virgin curls that had not endured
the roughness of a bristle brush.

I was not born yet. I was as remote as starlight.
It's hard for me to believe that
my parents made love
above an eccentric saint-painter
in a roomful of angels,
and I wasn't there.

But now I am. My mother is blushing.
This is the lovely thing about art.
It can bring back the dead.
It can wake the sleeping,
as it might have late that night
when my father and mother made love above Manuel,
who lay in the dark thinking holy, holy, holy.

RUNNING AWAY WITH GARY THE MATTRESS SALESMAN

Catherine Fraga

He beckons my husband and me over to the
king-sized mattresses as he fingers his cigarette pack
tucked into a shirt pocket/I really could not tolerate
a smoker but Gary cares about my comfort, my happiness/
offers amazing information about how crucial the
size of the springs are/the springs are everything/
he's not pushy/he gently invites me to go to sleep/
imagine I am sleeping on say this one/
how do you feel/he wants to know how I feel/he is
talking to me/waiting for my answer/it's the only thing
he cares about and now I just want him to leave
with me/I would follow him/even though he wears
pressed Wrangler jeans slightly belled at the bottom/
he know the ins and outs of comfort/I think he is
taken with me/I know he wants me to be happy/
it is a stroke of luck/
the Chiffons singing *he's so fine* on the store's radio/
my husband and me buying a mattress today from Gary.

Matthew Lane Brouwer

June 2013

CREATIVE WRITING 101

Matthew Lane Brouwer

I forget I know anything about writing poetry

I forget I have written 500 poems

I forget there is a box beneath my bed
with twenty dusty journals in it

I forget the binders in my desk
where I have stockpiled poems
like ICBM's

I forget my transcript has a line on it which reads
"Creative Writing"

I forget I know the definitions of terms like
heroic couplet and *nonrestrictive clause*

I forget there is an open mic

I forget there is a darkened room
where I have read 50 times

I forget that there are 50 people in it
with the candlelight of expectation in their eyes

I forget the compliments I have received
I forget that I would like to receive more

I forget the title of the book I'm writing in my head

I forget the vision of seeing it on some Barnes and Noble shelf

I pour my breaths into a glass with ice in it
and sip them slowly like vermouth
I study the whiteness of the walls

until the minutes halt their drip
I ask the poem if it thinks it knows
who I am

and it replies

I am not a birth certificate
nor the name written in the blank

I am not a bottle of formaldehyde
in which to place the heart

I am not the scalpel
nor the surgeon's well-trained hands

I am not a magistrate
nor the stone of his decrees

I am the pavilion through which the breeze
might freely blow

I am the hardwood floor
on which the wedding parties dance

I am the mesh through which the sun
can peek its skull

I am the lattice up which the climbing vine ascends

I am the dissipation of the cloud
into tiny drops of rain

I write down the last shape
I think it takes

Put out an empty glass
wait to see what it collects

MEMORY DRUG

Matthew Lane Brouwer

Their first use was with soldiers
those who woke in the night
in sweat
remembering the blood upon their arms
their buddies' final cries

Slept easy ever after

The people thought this was a miracle
their men had finally come home

And so the drug was approved

Next it was used on criminals
wiped out their pasts

So violent urges
became venomless snakes
that shriveled into dry skins

And death row devils
could lie down in city parks
watch children climb up jungle gyms

Next it was victims
until there was no one left to press charges

Then it was the junkies
and the streets became safe of petty crimes

We began to see that it was our memory
that was the enemy
The past our prison cell
we all sentenced ourselves to
and without it
we were finally free

Then it became prescription

any doctor could write for anyone
for nearly anything

A fight, a break up, a bad night of sex
distress was now an ailment
easily cured
like a case of strep

Then we said

Let's forget as much as possible
for this living is hard
and there is much to make us sad

We only want to remember pay raises
and ice cream socials

So we became addicted to amnesia
addicted to not having to remember pain

And then the president said

We can help you forget your history
your mothers and your fathers
and their mothers and fathers before them

There is much they did wrong
They gave your life so much pain

And so the drug got put in the water

And honestly
I don't really remember much of anything
after that

PLAYING WITH MATCHES

Matthew Lane Brouwer

Start with anything in your life
that is burning

Humans love to watch a thing
that is going down in flames

Compare it to a fireplace
to a device that leverages destruction
to keep something else alive

Tell us what happens
when the ash goes cold

How civilizations in the heart
become buried under arctic ice

Tell us what happens if it leaps beyond
its enclosure

Explain how Chicago burned down
when a cow kicked over a bucket of coals

How London was scorched to black dirt
by a boy playing with matches

That a whole world can be ignited
by one human being
who decides to be fully, openly, carelessly
alive

NSAA

August 2013
aka Lawrence Dinkins, Jr

DEVIL CAKE

NSAA

Temptation
I vowed I would resist
I bite my lower lip
I close my eyes and envision
Licking the icing
And with two fingers pinch the moist inside sweet
Lost in sugar high rush
I push it into my face with both hands
I try to put the whole thing in my mouth
Like my name is greedy
Eyes rolled backward
I taste it all at once
The bitter, sweet, salty
Swirl around the pleasure centers
Plunging me into diabetic shock
Causing hallucinations
I rub it all over
So that my entire body can sample
And stop long enough to eat the cherry slowly
And relish it like the nipple of the Virgin Mary
All of that softness
Taste so good, feels so good
I put my dick in it
And fucked the shit out of that dark chocolate
Soft and creamy pulls me in deeper
Compliments to the chef for creating such a wonderful
Editable masterpiece, you are truly a fine ass delight
When I thought it couldn't get any better
Then
We were joined by red velvet
Angel cake got jealous
So I invited her to join us
We made a sugar disaster area the size of Katrina
The police came, fire fighters, the mayor
I came so hard it sent me into convulsions

And I scream out, "Holy God in Heaven,
thank you black zombie Jesus!"
I open my eyes and see on the other side of the glass
A shocked older black, lady hand over her mouth, adjusting her wig
A little child, with his mom half covering his eyes
A clown halfway through making what looks like a balloon penis
I stand up fully nude in the display case
Covered in cake and sex
Raise my fist to the heavens and yell,
"Why does this happen every time I pass a bakery?!"

CLUTCH

NSAA

Woman
Sexy mamma
Easy rider
Sit here
Drive
Shift
Arch
Back
Pop
Clutch
Gear in first
Ride
'til the wheels come off
'til the engine drop
Hood buckles
Shaft breaks
Rubber burn
Run it into the ground
Until
Transmission slip
Engine knock
Until
Doors open
And fly off
Wipers turn on by themselves
Blinkers
Blink, blink, blinking
Hazards
Ding, ding, dinging
Muffler dragging
Sparks flying
Riding on rims
Find that gear
Grind, grind, grinding
Sputtering

Gyrating
Jerk, jerk, jerking
Black smoke
Rising
As we break down
In some dew covered vacant field
Some ditch
Some bed
With broken springs

NOT SO NICE LIKE

NSAA

I want to mess your hair up
But I want you to get it done first
All pretty like
Put flowers in it: Bright and cheerful
And make up the bed
With throw pillows: Fancy and plush
With three thousand thread count sheets: Pink and pleated
Covers: Turned down and tight
I want you to come to the door when I knock
And answer it politely
Red lipstick dressed in virgin white
Flowing like an earth goddess
Take me by the hand
Lead me into your private chamber
And let me make the Angels weep
Counting the sins we commit
As we rip away the covers
Your legs up: Propped with plush pillows
Embossed designs tattooing your under thigh
As we sweat into the sheets
Exploring each thread count intimately
As we wilt the flowers
Into a submissive fade
As I grab a handful of your hair
Like a horses mane
As I ride you into the sunset
Let me look at you
As we lay panting
With your hair all over your head
Looking like Patti Labelle after singing 15 gospel songs in a row
Looking like Tina Turner after rolling on the river
Looking like Aretha after getting R-E-S-P-E-C-T

Kelly Freeman

August 2013

Accompanied by "Just the Tip"

COVER ME

Kelly Freeman

Cover me
in kisses
warm and wet
miss nothing
Blanket me in penetrating stares
because I love the way you look at me
You will be my winter coat this eve my love
and I will wear you out.
Cover me
In words
Soft and sweet
Whisper nasty phrases
and empty promises
because it's all about the fantasy right?
I will only hold you accountable for pleasure
I will only promise you the moment
All I ask is that you
Cover me
In honey
In chocolate
In whipped cream
In rhythm...
Meet my hips at high noon
until the stroke of midnight.
Dance with me
until the music is no more than static
until the moon surrenders her position to the sun
Cover me.

MOVEMENT

Kelly Freeman

Over and over. Turn like the weather, beneath me.
Writhe.
Tremble and moan
Up and around
My legs stretched wide as arms for hugs
Sucking air in gasps
An Asthmatic's nightmare
has become a beautiful dream to me
in this movement.
Float...
Against me
Trade lotion for sweat
Blanket me in motion
Urgently.
Fingers find me
Faithful intruders
Coaxing me closer
hips surrender
finding rhythm in the guitar you play
I remember the sun when we started
Warm on my face
Rotation
The moon meets its twin fully now
Affirmation in a glance
Quivers and shakes
Arched
Wearing your hands as a belt
My body impatient to thrill
supresses nothing
Gives it all away to you.
Spills forth
Rain.

Molly Fisk

October 2013

THE FAITHFUL

Molly Fisk

Sometime during the night I woke, convinced
the familiar W of Cassiopeia overhead was merely
a random cluster of stars and morning was near,
though the clock said 1:46 and the sky was dark
as it gets inside a coat sleeve in November
when you're poking around, trying to find your scarf
and gloves. Smoke hangs over us during the day,
the sun a bleary eye, then melts at dusk
back to the valley. Fourteen California fires are half-
contained but rowdy: they jump the lines as soon
as heads are turned. Thus is the summer
of our discontent made ignominious winter, and we close
our bedroom windows, coughing. We're the lucky ones.
It's not our own houses burning. And we knew all along
global warming was coming. We're the offspring
of socialists, Communists, and skeptics: the ones
who, from the very first, believed.

STOKING THE FIRE AT 3:48

Molly Fisk

before there's any sign of morning and the air
when I go out for kindling is glassy cold.
I let the wood get wet and what's drying now

on the tiles catches slowly, sizzles like an animal
turning on a spit. I cancelled the paper long ago.
Now my old drafts are tinder, heat curls inflammatory

stanzas on 20-pound bond. I know it's absurd.
Not the pioneer-approved method.
When it comes to building fires, I'm exhausted

before I start. Half the wood is too big
for the stove's door and I have no axe. It's good
to know why everyone's so stern about tarps —

the best mistakes being educational but not fatal.
I tug open the gate and back through, even though
the blue wheelbarrow's tire is flat. You can't see this

in the dark but gray smoke is pouring from the chimney
now. I was a Girl Scout but you'd never know it,
throwing store-bought fire-starters in on top,

although they do catch, and half-finished sonnets light up
and the damp wood after a long while burns merrily,
like some perfect pile of birch logs Robert Frost thought up.

BEFORE I GAINED ALL THIS WEIGHT

Molly Fisk

I was so self-conscious I could barely
walk into town for fear people
would stare. I thought I was hideous,
unlovable. Now I want to shake
that poor girl, even though it wasn't
her fault, so afraid to be human —
rattle her cage of good grades, self-
tanning lotion and green eye-liner,
fast-acting depilatory cream, tell her
to smile for God's sake and kiss
the next boy she sees, life is shorter
than anyone imagines. Silver planes
plummet from clean skies, cancer gnaws
the marrow of even younger bones
than yours, wake up! There's still time!
Everything around you is unbelievably
beautiful.

Stan Zumbiel

October 2013

AMORAL AND GODLESS UNIVERSE

in movable letters.
A blue jeaned man
with the bucket of jumbled words, looks
up as if someone watches
from the white painted tower
where bells ring out on Sunday
morning sending vibrations through
rooftops and trees, beckoning
people to hear the word of God,
calling people to lay down
their sins, have souls as white as gloves
of young women.

Smoke rises, takes messages to
God, messages carried on the burning
flesh of small animals. The central ritual
involves singing, as if voices
go where smoke can't, as if
there were only one language that
can bridge the distance to God.
Archaic linguistic constructions
possess the secret.

He closes the glass cover,
picks up the bucket and returns
to the cramped office where
he pulls books from the bookcase,
makes notes, sits on a wooden
swivel chair and leans over a scarred
oak desk with drawers on each side.

The universe spins, searching for
itself, trying to discover what
belongs to the dead – memory, a bit
of earth, coincidences.

A window high up the wall
puts a pool of light on his papers.

Go to the edge. The descent isn't bad.
You don't need choirs of angels
to catch you. Your approaching
shadow is not what it seems.

CEYX AND ALCYONE

Stan Zumbiel

Beach walkers wander out of the fog—spirits materializing
suddenly then suddenly disappearing, faces pale
as drowned sailors. Some are lovers. Weep to see them silent,
unconnected, unable to tell their stories. You're perfectly
situated to witness the redemption of seabirds.

1.

Two walk barefoot, carrying their shoes. He
wears a tattered pea coat and blue jeans rolled to mid calf. She
wraps herself in a sweater, and wind blows her hair. They stop
to look at shells and parts of shells submerged in the wet sand.
Sandpipers run in the shallow foam, footprints disappearing
as they are made. He looks at the fog a hundred yards off shore,
lifts a piece of jagged driftwood as if he's Zeus, holds it like
lightning, and heaves it, making a storm among scattering
gulls. He runs with splashing laughter into the sea.

2.

She starts suddenly from a deep sleep weeping, grasping
the bed and seeking relief. There is no relief in the darkness,
only the continuation of dream, flickering images – a pale face
wrapped in kelp staring empty into the sky, black flies not swept
away by the wind, buzzing over a jellyfish stranded on the sand.
It's a dance, flies and sleeping girl facing birds darting from
the shallow surf, where endless circling constitutes a mating
ritual. The movement of his hips under water draws them in.

3.

Two migrating Elegant Terns who spent the night over
the Pacific, rest on the gently undulating waves green
in the new dawn. They have traveled and suffered,
have been punished and rewarded. They are the resurrection

of birds. In these wind swept days they would sing, if they could, a ballad with the sea for accompaniment. Morning after morning with the ritual of wings they perform the illusion of love.

ISAAC HILL CEMETERY

Stan Zumbiel

Blackbirds that nest among
dry tangled grasses
and crooked white stones
fly like spirits,
shoulders showing flames
as they escape into the morning.

Rain has settled everything:
dust on the graves of those
who look out over a lake
that was not here when they came;
the heat which glazes air
in opaque waves –
tree trunks and stones
released from stillness;
mud darkened by
westward pointing shadows of oaks
where no one walks in the morning
except me
straining to keep the quiet from my ears:
voices falling from leaves,
random sermons from weathered pulpits.

In trees the birds await my departure
while rain laid down carefully in the night
rises as mist
from lake, branch, and stone.

I feel soft tumbling in the earth
as the long dead turn to face the sun.

Shawn Pittard

December 2013
Accompanied by Clemon Charles

EL DESDICHADO

Shawn Pittard

The sea won't have me.
Ever since I sprouted legs

and walked ashore,
she's been haughty and aloof.

It hurts the most at twilight,
when the bright anemone

purples in her rock garden,
when the sun dissolves

inside the offshore fog,
leaves a silver skein

on the curve of her horizon.
When her gray tide

follows the moon onto the beach
and laps my feet and knees,

that's when I swim out,
out through her breaking waves,

down into her aching silence.
Only to be turned back again—

driven up and up
into the suffocating air.

DOMICILE

Shawn Pittard

I looked out the kitchen window
two years, almost three.

Each new morning brought a view
that sharpened—then dulled.

And each time I stepped away
to pour another cup of coffee

I came back to another man's life.

WHY WE'RE HERE

Shawn Pittard

Our father squints through trifocals,
searches for the eye of a fishhook.

Yellow goat horns ripple in a blue tattoo
across the tendons of my brother's forearm.

I catch myself humming a song
from my childhood religion.

We say we're here
to fish backcountry streams.

A father. Two prodigal sons.
Sorting gear and drinking coffee

on the tailgate of a pickup.
Listening for gaps in the silence.

ABOUT THE ARTISTS

Shawn Aveningo is an internationally published, multi-award-winning poet who hosts the Verse on the Vine™ poetry show. She's performed in San Francisco, Seattle, Portland, Sausalito, Sacramento and St. Louis. Her work has been published in over 50 anthologies, literary journals and e-zines, including *Pirene's Fountain, Nazar Look: Metric Conversions, Nefarious Ballerina, Convergence, Poetry Now, Tule Review, From the Four Chambered Heart: Tribute to Anaïs Nin* and *Haunted Waters Press Quarterly.* She's a Show-Me girl from Missouri, a Summa Cum Laude graduate from University of Maryland and a very proud mother of three. And she absolutely loves shoes – especially red ones! (www.RedShoePoet.com)

Lytton Bell has published three books (A Path Before Winter, 1998; The Book of Chaps, 2002 and Nectar, 2011) and was the winner in five national poetry contests. She has performed at many Northern California venues, including the Sacramento Poetry Center, The Grass Valley Center for the Arts, Luna's Café, Queen of Sheba, The Vox, Beatnik, Shine, Om Shan Tea (San Francisco) and The Book Collector, to name a few. Her work has appeared in over three dozen publications. Lytton's latest book *Nectar* can be found on Amazon.com.

Matthew Lane Brouwer's work bridges the worlds of spoken word and literary poetry to create a style that can be both evocative and subtle, enlivening and profound. He has performed in cities throughout the west and been featured in regional literary, performance, and visual arts showcases such as *Cirque, Phrasings,* and *Strands.* He teaches creative writing in Bellingham, WA public schools and facilitates a writing circle for people suffering chronic medical conditions. For more on Matthew's poetry and work visit: www.matthewbrouwerpoet.com.

Todd Cirillo was born of bastard lineage in the dark waters outside New Orleans. To this day, he retreats there – whenever heartbreak or hangover hit him. He is a co-founder, editor and publisher of the notorious Six Ft. Swells Press and one of the originators of the After-Hours Poetry movement. Cirillo is the author of five chapbooks of poetry and is a co-author of the infamous book, *Roxy.* Cirillo is another legendary poet who has been a featured reader all over the United States and an alleyway in Paris. Cirillo's new book, *Sucker's Paradise*, was released in October 2012. You can find him on youtube.com, at afterhourspoetry.com, or underneath the neons...somewhere.

Jack Donaldson is by profession a Registered Nurse, by heart a poet, essayist, and writer of lyrics and prose. His works are influenced by quantum physics, a lust for life, and the irony of the arrogance of man. Weaving the spoken word with guitar accompaniment he hopes to bring to the audience a pleasurable experience of cognitive contemplation and visceral harmony. He has performed at Luna's Cafe, Butch and Nellies, Mondo Bizarro, Fox and Goose, Old Ironsides, Torch Club, The Blue Lamp, Shine, and the True Love Cafe. His limited editions include *Contemplative Silence, Tranquility's Bay, So Much Time*, and *Life's Back Porch*. His current book of poetry and prose *Accretion* may be purchased as an eBook or dead wood version at Blurb.com.

Molly Fisk was born in San Francisco. She earned her B.A. from Radcliffe College / Harvard University, her M.B.A. from Simmons College Graduate School of Management, and began writing at the age of 35. She's the author of *The More Difficult Beauty* (Hip Pocket Press, 2010), *Listening to Winter* (Roundhouse Press/Heyday Books, 2000), *Terrain* (with Dan Bellm and Forrest Hamer, Hip Pocket Press, 1998), the letterpress chapbook *Salt Water Poems* (Jungle Garden Press, 1994) and two CDs of radio commentary: *Blow-Drying a Chicken* and *Using Your Turn Signal Promotes World Peace*. Molly has received fellowships in poetry from the National Endowment for the Arts, the California Arts Council, and the Marin Arts Council. She's won the Dogwood Prize, the Robinson Jeffers Tor House Prize in Poetry, the Billee Murray Denny Prize, the National Writer's Union Prize and a grant from the Corporation for Public Broadcasting. She serves as Poet Laureate of radio station KVMR-FM, Nevada City and recently appeared in the TEDxSanFrancisco event The Edge of What We Know.

Catherine Fraga teaches writing at Sacramento State University. Her poems have been widely published in numerous journals and anthologies. She has been nominated for a Pushcart Prize and has been the recipient of several poetry awards. Her book, *Running Away with Gary the Mattress Salesman*, is published by Poet's Corner Press.

Writing is **Kelly Freeman's** first love. It saved her life. She has been writing since she was 12 years old. Her father was a poet as well, and encouraged Kelly to write and write often. She has shared this attitude with her own children and they also write. Performing is just an added bonus. The ability to share her life experiences with others through poetry has been incredibly rewarding. She is so thankful for this gift.

Dr. Telemachos Greanias is psychologist, researcher, author, and lecturer. His work in the exploration of the human entity is effortlessly woven into his poetry. Upon reading his book *A Naked Greek* (originally published in 1972), we are taken on a journey of the human spirit and gently nudged to look inside our universal truths and perhaps ask ourselves the difficult questions in life. He is a man full of experience, with both humorous and equally poignant tales to share with his audience. Dr. Greanias has shared his poetry and stories with audiences at universities in Chicago and Northern California as well as more intimate venues of the Greater Sacramento Area. His articles and poetry have appeared in countless publications. His lifework is driven by "intellectual curiosity, the need to know, and wanting to serve, propelling [his] search for [him]self".

Patricia Hickerson was a Barnard College graduate, a Warner Bros. dancer, newspaper copy editor and *Penthouse* fiction writer with a broadside *At Grail Castle Hotel,* a chapbook *Dawn and Dirty,* a hard cover *Punk Me,* and poetry in *Echoes, Convergence, The Yolo Crow, Medusa's Kitchen, Rattlesnake Review, The Ophidian, WTF, Presa, Passager, Primal Urge, Tenpagespress.com* and lots of other places. Sadly, she passed away in 2013 and is dearly missed.

Jeff Knorr is the author of three books of poetry, *The Third Body* (Cherry Grove Collections), *Keeper* (Mammoth Books), and *Standing Up to the Day* (Pecan Grove Press). His other works include *Mooring Against the Tide: Writing Poetry and Fiction* (Prentice Hall); the anthology, *A Writer's Country* (Prentice Hall); and *The River Sings: An Introduction to Poetry* (Prentice Hall). His poetry and essays have appeared in numerous literary journals and anthologies including *Chelsea, Connecticut Review, The Journal, North American Review, Red Rock Review, Barrow Street,* and *Like Thunder: Poets Respond to Violence* *in America* (University of Iowa). Jeff has edited, judged, and been a visiting writer for various conferences and festivals. He was the founding co-editor and poetry editor of the *Clackamas Literary Review*. He has also been an invited judge for contests such as the DeNovo First Book Contest, the Willamette Award in Poetry and the Red Rock Poetry Award. He has appeared as a visiting writer at such venues and festivals as Wordstock, University of Pennsylvania's Kelly Writer's House, The Des Moines Festival of Literary Arts, and CSU Sacramento's Summer Writers Conference. He currently directs the River City Writer's Series at Sacramento City College. Jeff has been the Chair of the English department at Sacramento City College and he has also served on the Sacramento County Office of Education Arts Advisory Board. Jeff Knorr lives in Sacramento, California and is a professor of literature and creative writing at Sacramento City College.

Phillip Larrea is the author of two books, *We the People* (Cold River Press) and *Our Patch* (Writing Knights Press). He serves on the board of the Sacramento Poetry Center and hosts the reading series "Foam at the Mouth".

Cynthia Linville has lived in London, New York, San Francisco, and outside of Washington, DC but keeps coming back to live in her hometown of Sacramento. She has taught in the English Department at California State University, Sacramento since 2000 and has served as Managing Editor of *Convergence: an online journal of poetry and art* since 2008. She is active in the local poetry scene, hosting readings, and reading with the group Poetica Erotica, as well as on her own. A music aficionado with a theater background, she is usually out and about supporting the arts in Sacramento and in the San Francisco Bay Area. Her book of collected poems, *The Lost Thing*, is available from Cold River Press.

Laura Martin is a freelance writer/photographer whose features, essays, poetry and images have appeared in such publications as Sacramento magazine, Solano magazine, Via magazine, the San Jose Mercury News, the Boston Globe, the San Francisco Chronicle, Susurrus, The Tule Review, Late Peaches: Poems by Sacramento Poets, and Medusa's Kitchen. She was the grand prize recipient of the Second Annual Pat Schneider Poetry Contest in 2012 and was recently nominated for a Pushcart Prize for poetry. As an Amherst Writers and Artists affiliate, Laura leads private writing workshops in the Sacramento area.

Indigo Moor is a poet, playwright and author currently residing in Sacramento, CA. His second book of poetry, *Through the Stonecutter's Window*, won Northwestern University Press's *Cave Canem* prize. His first book *Tap-Root* was published as part of Main Street Rag's *Editor's Select Poetry Series*. His short plays, *Harvest, Shuffling* and *The Red and Yellow Quartet* all debuted at the 60 Million Plus Theatre's Spring Playwright's Festival. His stage play, *Live! at the Excelsior,* was a finalist for the *Images Theatre Playwright Award* and is being made into a full length film. A graduate of the *Stonecoast MFA Program*—where he studied poetry, fiction, and scriptwriting. Indigo is also a graduate member of the *Artist's Residency Institute* for Teaching Artists. He is the winner of the 2005 *Vesle Fenstermaker Prize for Emerging Writers,* a 2009 Pushcart Prize nominee and 2008 Jack Kerouac Poetry contest winner. Other honors include: finalist finishes for the *T.S. Eliot Prize, Crab Orchard First Book Prize, Saturnalia First Book Award, Naomi Long Madgett Book Award* and *WordWorks Prize.* Collaborative efforts include the *Artists Embassy Intl. Dancing Poetry Festival, the Livermore Ekphrastic Project* and the *Davis Jazz Arts Festival.*

Known as Lawrence Dinkins, Jr. during the day but at night known as the nefarious **NSAA,** he is the author/editor of *Open Mic Sketchbook* (2013), a quick look-in at the Mahogany Urban Poetry Series, one of Sacramento's oldest spoken word venues where Lawrence is a host. He has also released two spoken word CD's *Lightning in a Bottle 1* (2009) and *Lightning in a Bottle 2: NSAA's Revenge* (2013). Along with Ross Hammond, he is one half of Electropoetic Coffee, a poetry/musical duo that blends spoken word with guitar improvisation.

Shawn Pittard is a writer and teaching artist living in Sacramento, California. He's the author of two slender volumes of poetry, *Standing in the River*, winner of Tebot Bach's 2010 Clockwise Chapbook Competition, and *These Rivers* from Rattlesnake Press. He works as a California Poet in the Schools, coaching high school students toward meaningful poetry recitations for Poetry Out Loud: the National Recitation Contest and as a poet-in-residence integrating art and science. He has also written two screenplays, one with his brother Trent, and is always looking for a producer.

In 2010, **Allegra Silberstein** was named the first ever Poet Laureate of the City of Davis. A longtime Davis teacher (now retired), dancer, and philanthropist, Allegra is known widely for her work as coordinator for The Other Voice, a reading series that takes place at the UU Church of Davis, and for her support of local writers. Her poems have been published in *Poetry Depth Quarterly, The Yolo Crow, Blue Unicorn, Rattlesnake Press, Poetry Now, Iodine Poetry, Poetry of the New West, California Quarterly* and other journals. She has also placed poems in a variety of anthologies, including *The Sacramento Anthology: One Hundred Poems, Gatherings, A Woman's Place,* and *Where Do I Walk.* Her first chapbook, *Acceptance,* was published in 1999, and her book *In the Folds* was published by Rattlesnake Press in 2005. She is currently working on a full-length book of poems.

Brigit Truex has lived in the four quarters of the States since beginning her writing career. In each locale she has also established workshops to help others hone their prose and poetry as well, but her primary focus is on poetry. Her mixed ethnic background (French Canadian-Abenak/Cree and Irish) has been a theme she continues to explore in her work, approaching it from various angles. She has been published in various international literary journals and anthologies including *Atlanta Review, Contemporary Literary Review: India, Tule Review, Yellow Medicine Review* and others. In addition to three chapbooks, her latest book, *Strong as Silk: The Story of the Wakamatsu Tea and Silk Colony,* was just released in 2012 by Lummox Press. She is a board member of Wordcraft Circle of Native Writers and Storytellers and Native Writers Circle of the Americas.

Though born in Cincinnati, Ohio, **Stan Zumbiel** has spent most of his life in the Sacramento Valley, arriving in Auburn, CA in 1950, moving then to Lincoln before settling in Fair Oaks. He received degrees from American River College and CSUS. In January 2008, he received his MFA in Writing from Vermont College of Fine Arts. He started writing poetry while in the Navy and further cut his poetic teeth in workshops led by Mary Moore, Julia Connor and Susan Kelly-Dewitt. He served on the board of the Sacramento Poetry

Center for 25 years. In 2008 he retired after teaching middle school and high school English for 35 years. He currently writes in Fair Oaks where he lives with his wife Lynn. His poems have appeared in *Poet News*, *The Suisun Valley Review, Medusa's Kitchen, Nimrod, Off Channel, Late Peaches* and *Primal Urge*.

AT THE OPEN-MIC

Thank you to all of our Open-Mic Performers who added a wonderful sense of community to our show each month. Sometimes there were only two souls brave enough to sign up, and sometimes we had a dozen who couldn't wait to hit the stage. Either way, each one of them shared their stories, their imagination and their heart with all of us; and for that we were all enriched.

Inge Nibblett
Art Smith
Caroline Swanson
Wendy Williams
Hatch Graham
Taylor Graham
Kae Sable
David Iribarne
M.E. Miller
Moira Magneson
Jeremy Greene
Jim Nolt
Irene Lipshin
Lara Gularte
Eve Diaz
Regina Karsh
Charles Asher
Ashley Rose Smith
Monica Lopez
Tim Bellows
B.L. Kennedy
Jovan Mays
Destiny Page
Stan Ketchum

Wendy Williams

Jeremy Greene

Caroline Swanson

Jovan Mays

Taylor Graham

Hatch Graham

B.L. Kennedy

Jim Nolt

Lara Gularte

K'ae Sable

M.E. Miller

Inge Nibblett

Ashley Rose Smith

Regina Karsh

Art Smith

Tim Bellows

Charles Asher

Eve Diaz

Stan Ketchum

Monica Lopez

Irene Lipshin

Destiny Page

David Iribarne

Moira Magneson

Open Mic

Troy Myers

THROUGH THE LENS

Verse on the Vine™ has been quite the experience as both a photographer and a fellow artist. As much as I have been immersed in the arts, never had I quite the visceral experience that came with poetry in such a sovereign room. The Wine Gallery is magical in its own energy of visual stories peering down from the high, warmly lit walls. There are tales from painters, illustrators and photographers, some screaming their presence, some quietly waiting for that unique individual who feels the connection.

As the room would fill and the feature introduced, I'd often realize a very special blend of particular stories from the frames, melded into the tales from the poets. Ironically, more times than not, some symbiosis of quaintness would suddenly arise from the words spoken by the feature, or the open-mic, and a painting would come to life.

Or the opposite would happen, the textures, colors or subtleties of the images would inspire the story from the poet. The photographs, a glint of the passion from spoken word, would as splendidly reveal this harmony, captured by the thump of my camera's shutter. Freezing a moment, a word, an expression, was always the reward.

As Verse on the Vine™ continued to bring more outstanding talent to the room, my own observations changed. My 'through the lens' experience was changing. I found myself caught in a bit of dichotomy. It was more apparent than ever that I had to choose between listening to the poem and capturing a moment. It turned out that I couldn't shoot the guest poet and retain anything shared; I had to choose between the shot or the poem. This was a challenge. I always strived to get a better photograph, but I also needed the energy of the poet at just the right moment, catching them in action, in a moment of splendid or divine expression. I always went for the photo and listened as intently as I could, sometimes stealing the deeper meaning, hopefully capturing the poet's unique delivery.

It has been an honor and blessing to experience all these wonderful writers and their amazing stories. The work of my partner, Shawn Aveningo, in putting this series in motion and managing all of the talent that graced our stage, has been incredible and a pleasure sharing. The gift of word, as it turns out for this artist, has far greater meaning in my life by sharing a photographic perspective of spoken word, all from the incredible sharing called Verse on the Vine™.

~Robert R. Sanders

A NOTE FROM YVONNE

It has been my privilege to host this series, and I am thrilled at the growth of the event and community response to every show. It was always my hope that this event would give the wonderful family of poets in our area a place to share their amazing works and provide a bit of something special for the community of Folsom - and the success of this event is just that. Your hard work and the growth of this event has been a tribute to the very essence of what community means to me.

It has been such fun watching people from all walks of life come and enjoy every featured artist and share words true to their hearts as well. I have loved seeing people laugh and cry as words of pure feeling filled their hearts and souls and moved them to some emotion that could not be ignored. I have often wondered how many hours of conversation took place after each show because I am convinced that many people went home and shared some of the feelings that were stirred by one or more of the artists presenting the work of their heart.

The range and talent of each orator was a very precious gift and one that I will treasure forever - my heart felt thanks to each and every artist that took time to share words from their heart. I felt like I was surrounded by light for days after each event and could not keep a smile to myself. And to you, Shawn, how do I say thank you for everything that had to be done behind the scenes, for all the incredible moments that filled my heart and made hard times worth working out.

This group (this family) of friends, poets and wine enthusiasts has all been blessed because you were willing to open the door for all of us to walk through. As a result, we were able to share something truly beautiful and were blessed beyond measure. Thank you, Shawn for everything. May you continue to be equally blessed.

Yvonne Norgauer
Owner, Petra Vineyard Wine Gallery

ACKNOWLEDGEMENTS

"Another Sip" by Shawn Aveningo, first published in *National Library of Poetry: Best Poems of 1995.*

"Just Another Day" by Shawn Aveningo, first published in *She Has Something to Say.*

"In Diffused Light" by Allegra Silberstein, first published in *California Quarterly.*

"My Joseph" by Allegra Silberstein, first published in *One Dog Press.*

"Toward Galaxies" by Allegra Silberstein, first published in *Yolo Crow.*

"Old Woman With Springtime Eyes" by Allegra Silberstein, first published in *Song of the San Joaquin.*

"Whispers" by Jack Donaldson, first published in *Accretion,* Vol 1.

"The Shawl" by Jack Donaldson, first published in *So Much Time.*

"Cat Hospital" by Lytton Bell, first published in *Rattlesnake Review.*

"Notes at Dawn and Dusk" by Brigit Truex, first published in *Stong as Silk.*

"How to Seduce Me" by Cynthia Linville, first published in *Poetica Erotica,* Vol 1.

"How to Seduce Me" by Shawn Aveningo, first published in *Poetica Erotica,* Vol 1.

"Lake Tahoe, 2004" by Phillip Larrea, first published in *We the People.*

"So Unfair" by Phillip Larrea, first published in *Four Plays, We the People & Inspired Heart Anthology.*

"Allegra" by Phillip Larrea, first published in *Four Plays & Inspired Heart Anthology.*

"Last Call Improv" by Indigo Moor, first published in *Tap Root.*

"One Summer" by Indigo Moor, first published in *Through the Stonecutter's Window.*

"My Body is a Soul Suitcase" by Laura Martin, first published in *Soul of the Narrator*.

"Weekends, Early Riser" by Laura Martin, first published in *Soul of the Narrator*.

"Ketchup" by Laura Martin, first published in *Soul of the Narrator*.

"Braided Lives" by Catherine Fraga, first published in *Journal of New Hampshire Institute of Art*.

"Holy Art" by Catherine Fraga, first published in *South Coast Poetry Journal*.

"Running Away with Gary the Mattress Salesman" by Catherine Fraga, first published in *Suisan Valley Review*.

"Creative Writing 101" by Matthew Lane Brouwer, first published in *The Gospel According to Matthew*.

"The Faithful" by Molly Fisk, first published in *Culture Weekly*.

"Stoking the Fire at 3:48" by Molly Fisk, first published in *Culture Weekly*.

"Before I Gained All This Weight" by Molly Fisk, first published in *Culture Weekly*.

"Issac Hill Cemetery" by Stan Zumbiel, first published in *Off Channel*.

"El Desdichado" by Shawn Pittard, first published in *Standing in the River*.

"Domicile" by Shawn Pittard, first published in *Standing in the River*.

"Why We're Here" by Shawn Pittard, first published in *Spillway 17*.

For the past two years, The Poetry Box™ and Petra Vineyard have presented Verse on the Vine™, a poetry series, hosted by Shawn Aveningo, featuring talented and highly acclaimed poets from the Northern California Region and beyond.

We invite the community to come enjoy poetic musings to stir the senses. Laugh, Cry, Share, and Feel as poets share their favorite works. Enjoy the superb wines of Petra Vineyard surrounded by the wonderful art gracing the walls of the gallery.

We encourage everyone to bring his or her own poetry to share at the open-mic. All forms of spoken word are welcome here!

Petra Vineyard's Wine Gallery is located at
627 Sutter Street, Folsom, CA 95630

Please visit **www.VerseOnTheVine.com** for:

Show Schedule
Upcoming & Past Featured Performers
Series Location Updates
Gallery of Photos from All the Shows
Purchasing Additional Books
Newsletter & Event Notifications

And Feel Free to Email Us at Shawn@thePoetryBox.com.

Made in the USA
San Bernardino, CA
17 November 2013